MY
BABY BOY
RECORD BOOK

This book belongs to

_____

_____

I'm on the way!

When Mom learned that I was on the way _____

_____

_____

_____

What Mom said to Dad _____

_____

_____

_____

How Dad reacted _____

_____

_____

_____

I am expected to arrive on this date _____

My first portraits

From the ultrasound scan it was learned that _____

_____

_____

While waiting for me, Mom and Dad pictured me as

_____

_____

What Mom and Dad called me when I was in her tummy

_____

The hopes and dreams of my parents _____

_____

_____

_____

My first ultrasound

Mom with baby bump

My first photograph

I WAS BORN ON

_____

AT THIS TIME

_____

Here I am!

My weight _____

My height _____

I was born at _____

_____

The doctor and midwife who were there _____

_____

_____

The most vivid memory of the day was _____

_____

_____

_____

_____

What they said about me...

Mom's first words _____

_____

_____

_____

Dad's first words _____

_____

_____

_____

The hopes and good wishes of relatives and friends _____

_____

_____

_____

_____

_____

My name

I am called _____

_____

My name was chosen by _____

_____

_____

_____

What it means _____

_____

_____

_____

My nickname is _____

_____

_____

My identikit

Color of eyes
_____

_____

Color of hair
_____

_____

Complexion
_____

_____

Distinguishing features
_____

_____

_____

_____

What is my sign?

My zodiac sign is _____

The characteristics of this sign are _____

_____

_____

_____

_____

According to Chinese astrology I am a

☆ dog   ☆ dragon   ☆ horse   ☆ monkey   ☆ ox   ☆ rabbit

☆ goat   ☆ rooster   ☆ snake   ☆ tiger   ☆ pig   ☆ rat

The characteristics of this sign are _____

_____

_____

_____

Precious memories

The hospital bracelet

A lock of hair

My photographs

Mom and Dad

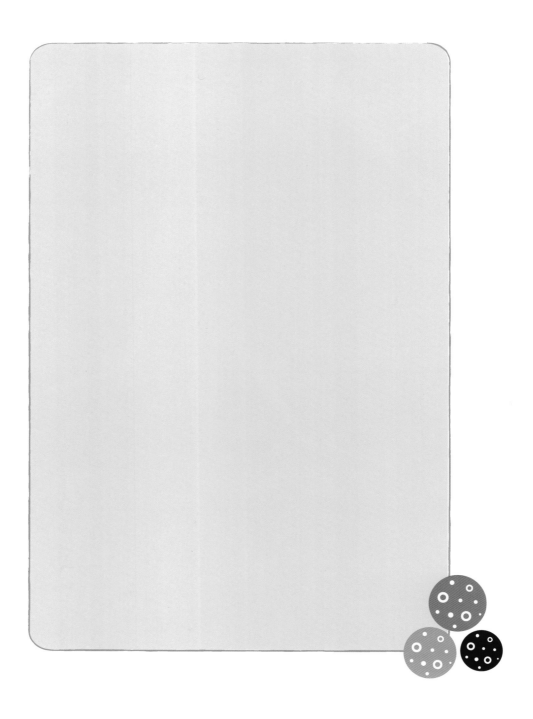

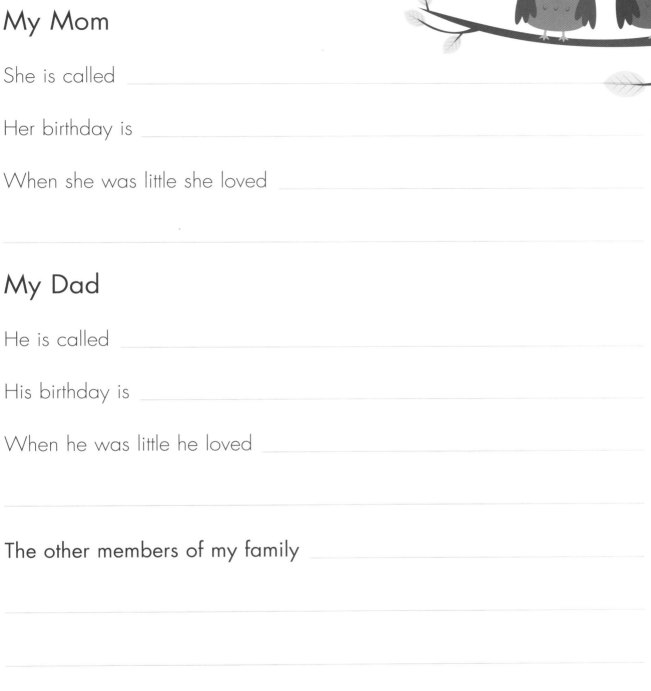

My Mom

She is called _____

Her birthday is _____

When she was little she loved _____

_____

My Dad

He is called _____

His birthday is _____

When he was little he loved _____

_____

The other members of my family _____

_____

_____

_____

_____

They say I look like...

Eyes
_____

_____

Mouth
_____

_____

Nose
_____

_____

Hair
_____

_____

Ears
_____

_____

Mom's
family tree

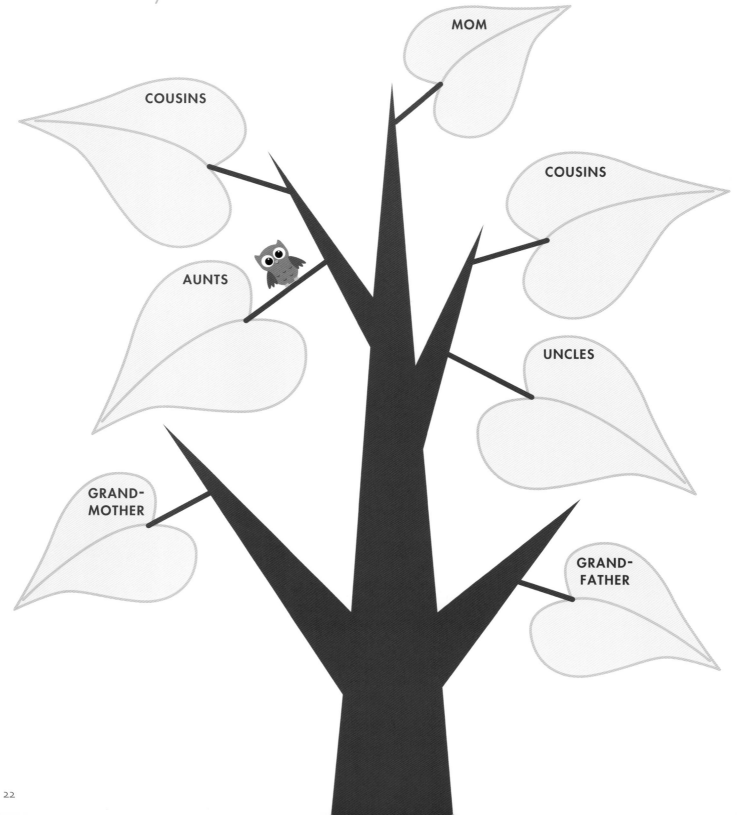

MOM

COUSINS

COUSINS

AUNTS

UNCLES

GRAND-
MOTHER

GRAND-
FATHER

Dad's family tree

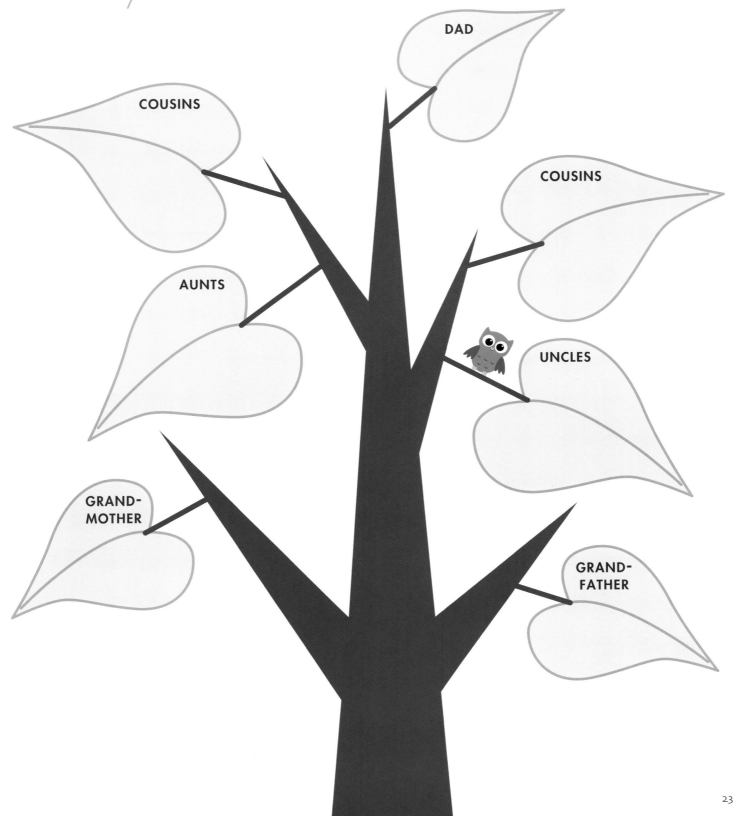

DAD

COUSINS

COUSINS

AUNTS

UNCLES

GRAND-MOTHER

GRAND-FATHER

Returning to my origins

Every tree has roots: here is what I have discovered about the origins of

my family _____

_____

_____

_____

_____

_____

My ancestors

THE DATE
I CAME HOME

My first photograph at home

My first address

While I was on the way home

Who was waiting for me

My little bedroom

How my room is decorated _____

_____

_____

_____

_____

Around me are these gifts from loved ones _____

_____

_____

_____

_____

_____

See how I'm growing!

WEIGHT CHART

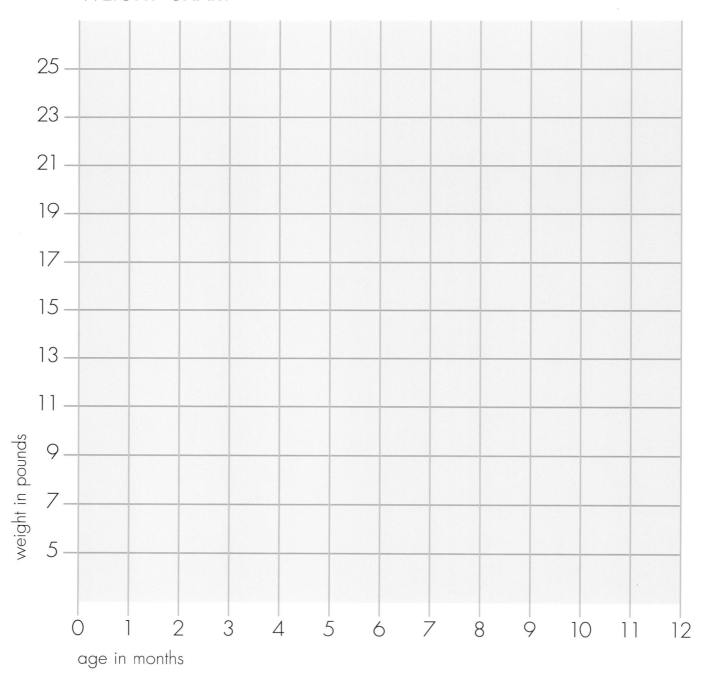

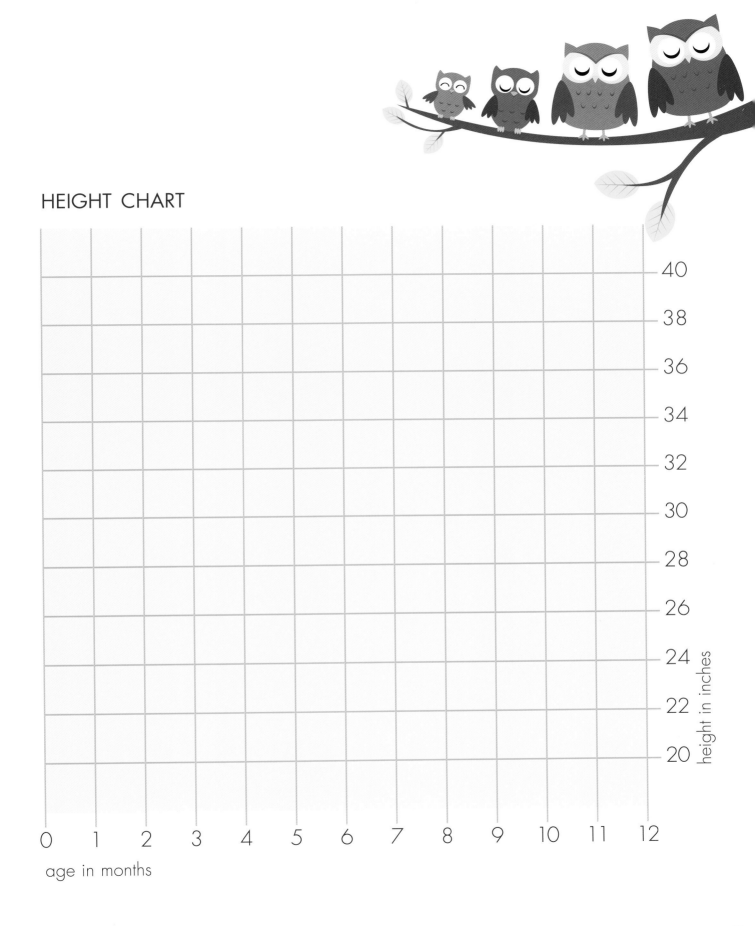

HEIGHT CHART

height in inches

40
38
36
34
32
30
28
26
24
22
20

0 1 2 3 4 5 6 7 8 9 10 11 12

age in months

Waking up

Am I an early bird or a sleepyhead? _____

_____

_____

_____

How I show I've woken up _____

_____

_____

_____

As soon as I open my eyes, I immediately _____

_____

_____

_____

My food is ready

My first solid food _____

_____

_____

Mom's recipes _____

_____

_____

_____

My favorite food _____

_____

_____

I don't like _____

_____

_____

The bath is ready

My first time in the bath _____

_____

_____

_____

How I reacted _____

_____

_____

_____

In the bath I play with _____

_____

_____

_____

Sweet dreams

My first whole night's sleep _____

_____

_____

_____

To go to sleep I need _____

_____

_____

_____

My favorite lullaby _____

_____

_____

_____

_____

My teeth come through

My first tooth came through _____

How I reacted to my new tooth _____

_____

_____

TOP ROW

LEFT
SIDE

RIGHT
SIDE

BOTTOM ROW

About the doctor

My doctor _____

The first time I went to the doctor _____

_____

_____

My blood group _____

Vaccinations _____

_____

_____

My first illnesses _____

_____

_____

My first appearance in public

Our family's first walk took place _____

_____

_____

How I reacted _____

_____

_____

The people I met said to me _____

_____

_____

My favorite places are _____

_____

_____

_____

A world to explore

The first time that:

I traveled by car _____

_____

I took a train, an airplane or a ship _____

_____

I went on holiday with my family _____

_____

I saw the sea _____

_____

I felt the snow _____

_____

There's always a first time

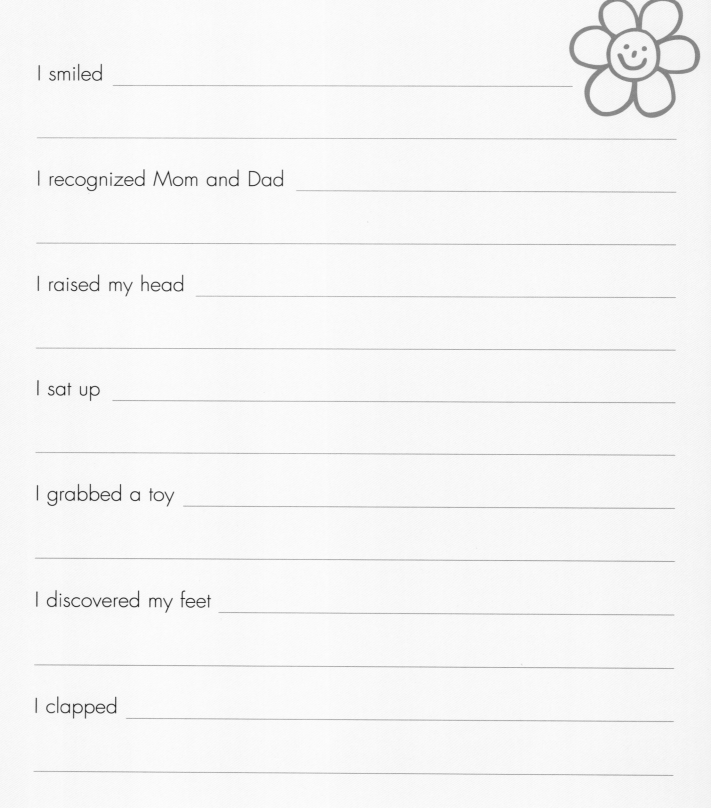

I smiled _____

_____

I recognized Mom and Dad _____

_____

I raised my head _____

_____

I sat up _____

_____

I grabbed a toy _____

_____

I discovered my feet _____

_____

I clapped _____

_____

On the move!

I started crawling _____

_____

I stood up on my own _____

_____

I wore my first "grown-up" shoes _____

_____

I made my first steps with a little help _____

_____

I walked on my own for the first time _____

_____

I started dancing _____

_____

I ran on ahead on my own _____

_____

A special day

Event
_____

_____

_____

Who was there
_____

_____

_____

_____

_____

An unforgettable memory
_____

_____

_____

_____

_____

My hand print

The size of my hand:

In the last 12 months…

Mom and Dad have never forgotten the time when I

What I learned to do this year

How much I have grown in one year

WEIGHT _____   HEIGHT _____

My personality

Happy birthday!

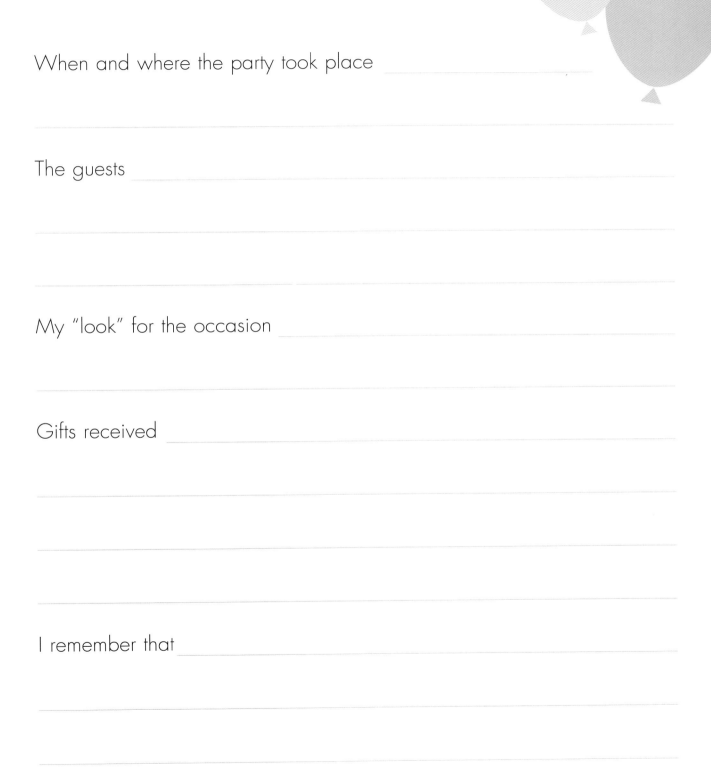

When and where the party took place

The guests

My "look" for the occasion

Gifts received

I remember that

There's always a first time

I built a tower

I tried to get dressed on my own

I ate on my own

I threw a ball in the air

I jumped

My new experiences

Famous first words

The first word I spoke was

How I pronounced it

I said "Mom" for the first time

I said "Dad" for the first time

My favorites

Fairy tale _____

_____

Song _____

_____

Toy _____

_____

Cartoons _____

_____

Stuffed toy _____

_____

Game _____

_____

Garment _____

_____

The thing that makes me happiest

The thing that upsets me most

The thing that comforts me

A special day

Event

Who was there

An unforgettable memory

My hand print

The size of my hand:

_____

In the last 12 months...

Mom and Dad have never forgotten the time when I _____

_____

_____

_____

What I learned to do this year _____

_____

_____

How much I have grown in one year

WEIGHT _____   HEIGHT _____

My famous sayings _____

_____

_____

_____

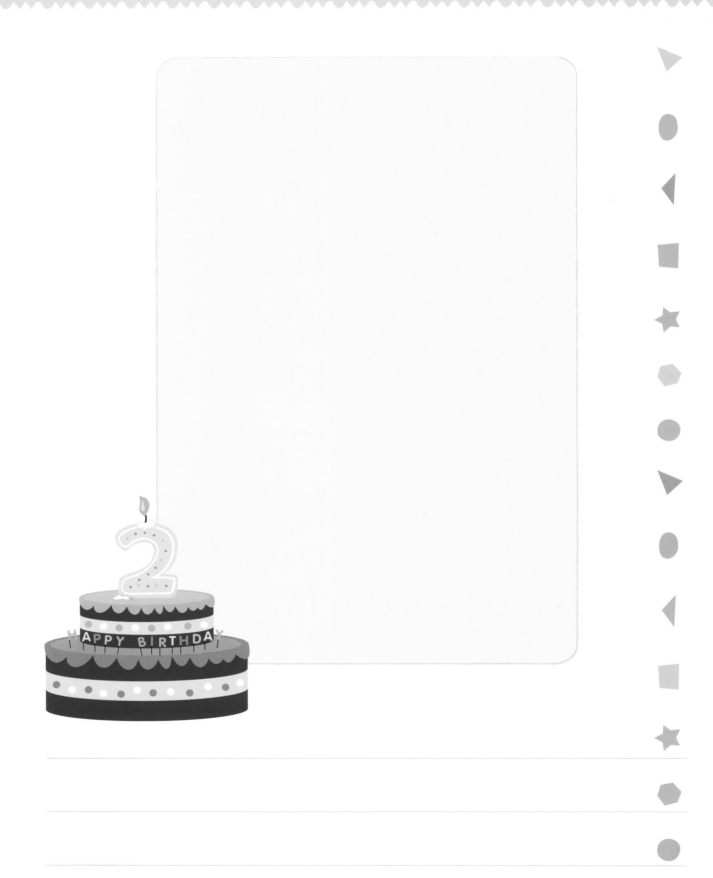

Happy birthday!

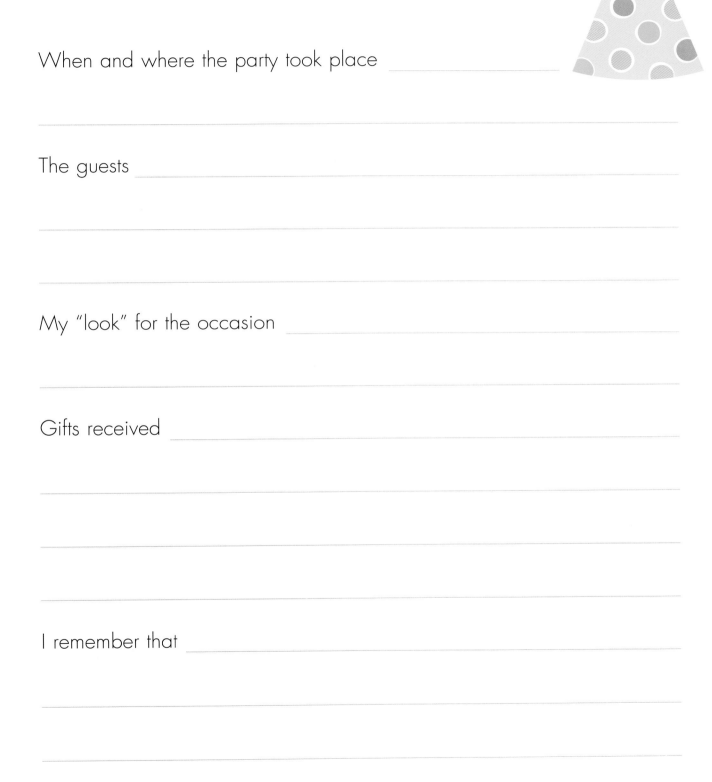

When and where the party took place _____

_____

The guests _____

_____

_____

My "look" for the occasion _____

_____

Gifts received _____

_____

_____

_____

I remember that _____

_____

_____

There's always a first time

I stopped wearing diapers _____

_____

_____

I drew a circle _____

_____

_____

I recognized colors _____

_____

_____

I counted up to 5 _____

_____

_____

I brushed my teeth myself _____

_____

I rode a tricycle

I dressed on my own

I used my own name

A new experience

Friends...

My friends are called _____

_____

_____

_____

_____

_____

These are the games I play with them _____

_____

_____

_____

_____

_____

My favorites

Fairy tale

Song

Toy

Cartoons

Stuffed toy

Game

Garment

The thing that makes me happiest _____

_____

_____

The thing that upsets me most _____

_____

_____

The thing that comforts me _____

_____

A special day

Event

_____

_____

_____

Who was there

_____

_____

_____

_____

An unforgettable memory

_____

_____

_____

_____

A drawing of my hand following the outline with a marker pen

The size of my hand:

_____

In the last 12 months...

Mom and Dad have never forgotten the time when I _____

_____

_____

_____

Something I learned to do this year _____

_____

_____

How much I have grown in one year

WEIGHT _____   HEIGHT _____

Something really silly that I did _____

_____

_____

_____

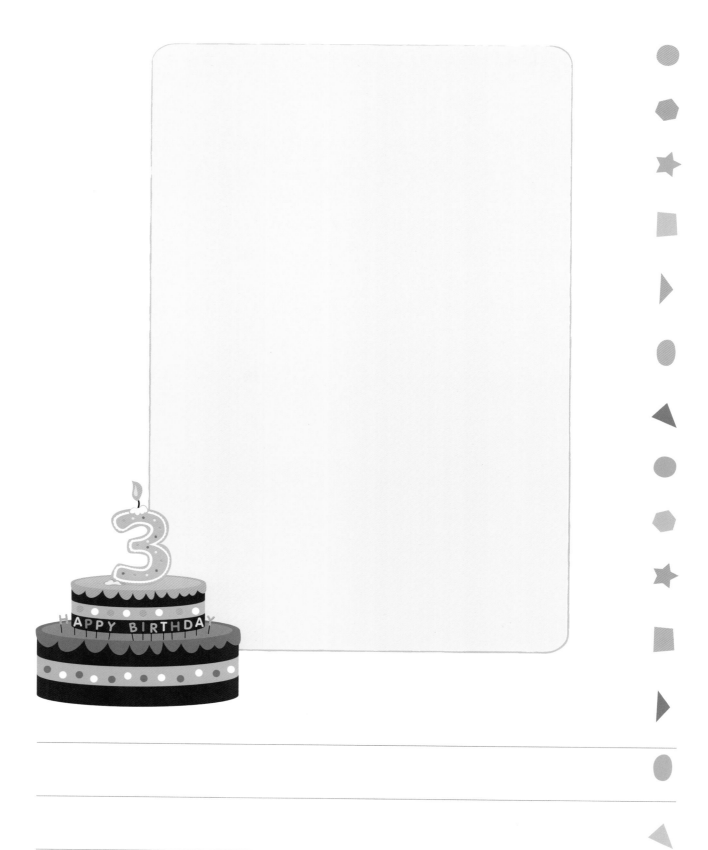

Happy birthday!

When and where the party took place _____

_____

The guests _____

_____

_____

My "look" for the occasion _____

_____

Gifts received _____

_____

_____

I remember that _____

_____

_____

There's always a first time

I drew a picture of an animal _____

_____

I went to a friend's party _____

_____

I chose my clothes in the morning _____

_____

I wrote my own name _____

_____

I stopped using a pacifier _____

_____

_____

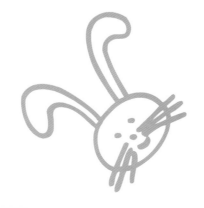  

My first time at preschool

The teachers

My favorite games

My reactions

Friends...

My new friends are called _____

_____

_____

_____

With them I play these games _____

_____

_____

_____

My best friend is _____

My best friend's birthday is _____

With my best friend I play _____

_____

_____

_____

My best friend

My favorites

Fairy tale _____

Song _____

Toy _____

Cartoons _____

Stuffed toy _____

Game _____

Garment _____

The thing which makes me happiest _____

_____

The thing which upsets me most _____

_____

The thing that comforts me _____

_____

A special day

Event

_____

_____

_____

Who was there

_____

_____

_____

_____

_____

A special memory

_____

_____

_____

_____

_____

Editorial management
VALERIA MANFERTO DE FABIANIS

Design
MARINELLA DEBERNARDI

Editorial assistant
GIADA FRANCIA

PHOTO CREDITS
123RF: pages 18, 20, 22, 23, 24, 31, 48, 50, 64, 66, 80, 82
Marinella Debernardi/Archivio White Star: pagg. 17, 34, 35
iStockphoto: pages 1, 3, 4, 6, 7, 8, 9, 10, 11, 12, 15, 16, 17, 21, 25, 27, 28, 29, 32, 33, 35, 37, 38, 39, 40, 41, 42, 43, 44, 45, 46, 47, 49, 51, 52, 53, 55, 56, 57, 58, 59, 60, 61, 62, 63, 65, 67, 68, 69, 71, 72, 73, 74, 75, 76, 77, 78, 79, 81, 83, 84, 85, 86, 87, 88, 89, 91, 92, 93, 94, 95, 96
Minimil/Getty Images: pages 2, 34, 36, 90

WS White Star Publishers® is a registered trademark
property of De Agostini Libri S.p.A.

© 2015, 2016 De Agostini Libri S.p.A.
Via G. da Verrazano, 15 - 28100 Novara, Italy
www.whitestar.it - www.deagostini.it

Translation and Editing: Rosetta Translations SARL

Revised edition

ISBN 978-88-544-1022-0
1 2 3 4 5 6   20 19 18 17 16

Printed in China